THE DEEP PHILOSOPHY GROUP

History, Theory, Techniques

Second Edition (2019)

Loyev Books

THE DEEP PHILOSOPHY GROUP

History, Theory, Techniques

Second Edition (2019)

Articles by:

    RAN LAHAV

    MICHELE ZESE

    FRANCESCA D'UVA

    MASSIMILIANO BAVIERI

    KIRILL REZVUSHKIN

    STEFANIA GIORDANO

    SEBASTIAN DROBNY

    SERGEY BORISOV

Edited by: Ran Lahav

ISBN: 978-1-947515-03-1

Copyright © 2019 Ran Lahav. All Rights Reserved
Cover photographs © Sergey Borisov and Michele Zese

Loyev Books
philopractice.org/web/loyev-books
1165 Hopkins Hill Road, Hardwick, Vermont 05843
USA

Contents

What is Deep Philosophy? *Ran Lahav*	1
The birth of Deep Philosophy *Michele Zese*	12
The structure of a session *Francesca D'Uva*	23
Procedures for studying texts *Massimiliano Bavieri*	37
Perspectives on inner depth *Kirill Rezvushkin*	49
Precious moments *Stefania Giordano*	65
The philosophical polyphony *Sebastian Drobny*	72
What is Recollection? *Sergey Borisov*	90
About the authors	99

Loyev Books

WHAT IS DEEP PHILOSOPHY?

Ran Lahav

In one sense, Deep Philosophy is the name of our group. In another sense, Deep Philosophy is way of doing philosophy. It is, more specifically, a contemplative way of philosophizing which our group practices.

Deep Philosophy as a group

Deep Philosophy Group is an international group of philosophers who are committed to doing philosophy in a contemplative way, using not just our abstract thinking but a deeper dimension of ourselves. As part of the tradition of Western philosophy, we reflect on fundamental issues of life and reality, but unlike the intellectual discourses of mainstream academic philosophy, in deep philosophy we reflect from our inner depth.

Our Deep Philosophy group was born on September 3, 2017, in the tiny village of Brando near Torino, Italy. This was the last day of an international philosophical-contemplative retreat which I organized with the help of my two friends, Michele Zese, whose family owns the retreat house, and Stefania Giordano, a colleague and friend who had been dreaming of organizing philosophical retreats for a long time.

The village of Brando is surrounded by Mediterranean forest and is situated on the side of a steep mountain, several kilometers from the picturesque town of Coazze – a perfect place for a quiet contemplative activity. It was a weekend retreat. Almost twenty people from several countries attended, and most of them left on Sunday afternoon. On Monday morning, six of us remained in the house.

We were sitting around a long table in the kitchen of Michele's beautiful house, a truly international group of people from Italy, Germany, Russia, Austria, and I from the USA (and Israel, where I grew up). We all had a previous acquaintance with philosophy, as well as with the philosophical practice movement which attempts to make philosophy relevant to the general public. But it was clear to us that this had not been an ordinary philosophical event. It had been nothing less than a demonstration of the remarkable power of philosophy to touch life and inspire it.

The philosophical retreat that had just ended had been intense and inspiring. It gave us all a sense of inner awakening, as well as of togetherness with each other. It showed us how philosophy can be more than abstract university lectures, more than opinionated arguments or logical analyses, more than a tool for solving problems. It demonstrated the power of philosophy to inspire a personal journey into one's inner depth, in togetherness with companions.

We were still under the influence of this intense experience as we were sitting around the table, talking quietly, thoughtfully, enjoying each other's company, reminiscing. Somehow the idea came up to use this experience as a basis for a general approach to doing philosophy. And once the idea was articulated in words, we all embraced it enthusiastically.

That morning we formulated a draft of our nascent vision. After going back home, we continued to communicate online and discuss it. We soon started conducting experimental skype sessions and working to enrich and consolidate our approach – our formats of interaction, our techniques and procedures, and our theoretical ideas.

This was the beginning of a process which is still continuing today, two years later, with marvelous creativity, productivity, and togetherness. Through this process we have developed a rich arsenal of philosophical exercises and techniques and a solid theoretical basis, all of which are elements in the approach we call "Deep Philosophy." We have been offering online sessions to people around the world, and giving workshops and retreats in several countries. New people joined our group, and we have ambitious plans for the future.

Deep Philosophy as an approach

The approach we call Deep Philosophy is born out of the yearning for realness, for truth and authenticity, in other words out of the yearning to get in touch with the foundation of life and reality. The exploration of fundamental life-issues falls in the domain of philosophy, but mainstream philosophy usually does so in an abstract way remote way. The philosophy we find at universities does not satisfy the yearning to touch life in its realness.

Deep Philosophy is a form of philosophy that refuses to remain on an abstract level, and seeks to touch reality in a personal way. Like many other human activities, it cannot be captured with a simple definition, but we can roughly characterize it in the following way:

To do Deep Philosophy is to reflect on basic issues of life and reality from our inner depth, in togetherness with our companions.

"Inner depth" is obviously a metaphor, and although it is difficult to define it in words, it is easier to understand it by consulting our personal experience. Most of us have experienced moments in which an insight or understanding appeared in our minds, moving us and inspiring us. The insight itself was not necessarily very clever or new, but it felt different from ordinary thoughts – precious, moving, elevating. It probably felt unexpected and surprising, as if originating not from ourselves, not from our ordinary mind but from a different part of our being, from some hidden source that is more primordial and central within us. It may have been accompanied by a sense of inner silence, of wonder and marvel, of realness, or plenitude. Clearly, a different dimension of our being has been touched and aroused.

This is a common example of the experience of understanding from our *inner depth*. We may say, then, that inner depth is an aspect of our being which lies beyond our ordinary state of mind, and which goes beyond our normal psychological patterns of thinking and feeling. It is, more specifically, a central aspect of our being, an inner fountain of understanding or awareness which projects, when awakened, to our entire being. Correspondingly, *deep understandings* are those insights that appear in our inner depth and awaken it, at least momentarily.

The notions of inner depth and deep understanding are central to what we call Deep Philosophy. The vision that guides our group is that it is possible to do philosophy from our inner depth, to reflect on fundamental issues of life from this deeper dimension within us. We value "deep" philosophizing very highly because it has the power to open us to broader horizons of understanding, beyond our normal intellectual thinking, and to impact our life profoundly, helping us on the road towards gradual self-transformation.

The pillars of Deep Philosophy

In order to sharpen our vision, we have formulated what we call The Pillars of Deep Philosophy, which are the essential ideas on which Deep Philosophy is based. Essential – because if any of them is missing, the practice is no longer Deep Philosophy. One may formulate these essential pillars in different ways, but it is best to see them as made of five concepts: yearning for realness, depth, giving voice, philosophy, and togetherness.

1. *Yearning for realness*: I encounter the first pillar when I yearn for truth, for authenticity, for ultimate reality, for the foundation or the heights, or (since these words have been over-used) for what we call "realness." When I yearn for realness I do not seek pleasurable experiences or happiness for myself, I do not try to satisfy my curiosity or interests. A yearning has little to do with satisfying desires or needs. It is more like love than desire: Like a lover who adores

his beloved (not his own experiences!) so that his heart "goes out" to her, likewise when I yearn for realness I move beyond myself and my self-interest, towards what is precious, real, true, fundamental. A yearning, like love, is an act of devotion, going-beyond oneself, and self-giving.

Deep Philosophy is born out of this yearning. Without this yearning, with only a desire for satisfactory experiences, there can be no Deep Philosophy.

2. *Inner Depth*: I sense realness in certain special states of mind, which are fundamentally different from my ordinary everyday moments (although the distinction is not sharp, and is sometimes a matter of degree and mixture). These special states have a special quality of inner unity, intense presence, fullness. They involve my whole being and not just an isolated thought or feeling, and I experience them as originating from an unfamiliar source within me, or even from outside my usual self. They are often accompanied by a sense of preciousness, of plenitude, of realness. In comparison, ordinary moments are fragmented, half-conscious, dull.

In this sense, those experiences are special not just in *what* I experience but in *how* I experience, in other words "where" within me I experience them, or which "dimension" of my being is activated. We call this inner dimension, which is usually dormant, and which is awakened only in those special moments, "inner depth."

This distinction between the deep and the superficial is crucial for Deep Philosophy, because it means that we must change our normal states of mind. Our usual mental states are not enough, and to do Deep Philosophy we must use methods – contemplative, poetic, etc. – to change them.

3. *Thinking-from (giving voice)*: When we seek realness, our aim is not just to feel and experience, but also to think and understand. Our path is philosophical, which means that it is based on understanding ideas. There is nothing wrong with deep experiences without understanding, as in meditation or spiritual music, but this is not Deep Philosophy.

However, our normal discursive thinking – theorizing, analyzing, opinionating, discussing – is not appropriate. It activates only a specific intellectual function of our mind, and not our inner depth. Discursive thinking has the structure of thinking-about: I think "about" some object of thought (real or imaginary, material or abstract, present or past). Metaphorically, I place before my mind an object of thought, and I inspect it as if I was an external observer. This "aboutness" relationship means that I am separate from the reality which I inspect, so that I am remote and uninvolved. It cannot bring me in touch with realness, which is the goal Deep Philosophy, but only allow me to think "about" it from a distance, from the outside. Thus, as long as I think and speak in the "aboutness" (discursive) mode, I cannot think from my inner depth and do Deep Philosophy.

The alternative is to think "from" the reality of our inner depth instead of about it, which is a very different kind of thinking. Metaphorically, I do not "inspect" reality in my mind, but rather "listen" inwardly to the way reality resonates within me, to the way it expresses itself in me. I think and speak *from* my reality and give voice to its realness, letting it manifest itself within me.

4) *Philosophy*: There are different ways to use words to get in touch with the realness of reality, among them poetry and myth. But our way is philosophical, which means that our goal is not just to experience reality but to understand it. Therefore, we work with philosophical ideas and understanding, which are powerful way to explore fundamental reality. Without the attempt to understand reality philosophically, a practice is not Deep Philosophy, as valuable as it might be.

For a philosophical understanding of reality and its realness, we must speak and think in the language of fundamental reality. Such a language cannot be limited to specific things, specific people, specific facts or events, because these are objects of thinking-about. The language of fundamental reality is fundamental ideas before they have been objectified into specific objects, which is precisely the language of philosophy. Deep Philosophy is, therefore, a philosophical exploration or discourse that uses thinking-from our inner depth.

In this exploration, I involve my own deep understandings or "voice," as well as the voices of my companions and of past philosophers. I do not limit myself to the way reality resonates in me personally, but include the way it resonates in human reality in general.

5) *Togetherness*: It is possible to practice Deep Philosophy individually, through individual contemplation, but this practice has its limitation. As long as I remain within myself and my world, as long as I limit myself to my own ideas, I do not step outside myself to take part in the broader horizons of understanding reality. In Deep Philosophy I therefore put myself in a togetherness of thinking, so that I am no longer the only creator and owner of my thinking. I now resonate with my companions and

with a philosophical writer, so that my thinking is part of a larger horizon of thinking, part of a richer polyphony of a fuller reality.

These five pillars may seem like a doctrine, but in fact they do not make any claim about life or reality. For us they are tools that orient us in our work, and that help us conduct our open-ended exploration. Indeed, our group members are not expected to embrace them as an authority. They serve as pointers to the general direction in which we are currently walking together, and we know that they may change in the future as we go along. As such, these five pillars are for us not an end-point but seeds for further enrichment and development.

THE BIRTH OF DEEP PHILOSOPHY

Michele Zese

Our Deep Philosophy group was born in our first philosophical-contemplative retreat in Brando, after several days of intense activities. In this chapter, I would like to describe how our story began.

The birth of the idea

Let me first go back a few months earlier, to a previous philosophical event which took at the end of April 2017. Ran Lahav, with the help of Stefania Giordano, organized a philosophical-contemplative retreat in Liguria, in the west of Italy. At that time, I knew very little about philosophical contemplation, but I had been fascinated by the idea since attending a lecture about it by Ran Lahav in Torino (Turin), in 2016. And so, when I happened to see a Facebook announcement of the Liguria retreat, I decided to participate.

It turned out that Ran had found a small house which belonged to friends of friends, not very far from my hometown. The house was located in a beautiful mountainous area, surrounded by wood. I remember vividly the difficulty to find the house. I had to park my car on the side of the small country road and walk downhill on a steep driveway for about ten minutes through trees and bush. When I finally found the place, I was impressed by the peaceful atmosphere. The participants all seemed to speak and behave in a contemplative mood, something that was totally new for me.

It was during that retreat that I met Ran and Stefania for the first time. And it was there that we started discussing the possibility of holding another retreat in the north of Italy. I understood somehow that Ran was looking for a different retreat place, so I suggested using my late grandfather's house, in the village of Brando, not far from the city of Torino. Less than five months later the idea became a reality, when we organized a new philosophical-contemplative retreat with almost twenty participants from several countries.

Brando is a tiny village in the northwest of Italy, on the feet of the Alps Mountains. Its location is ideal for this kind of retreat. It consists of a handful of houses surrounded by wood. Conveniently, Brando is accessible to international travelers – it is less than two hours away from the cities of Torino and Milano, yet it is situated in the midst of a quiet and serene landscape.

The structure of the sessions

We started our retreat on Thursday morning, August 30, 2017. The activity was intense. Every day we held a morning session and an afternoon session. Sessions were based on the format of the philosophical-contemplative companionship which had been developed a few years earlier by Ran Lahav and practiced in previous events in several countries.

We began each session by reading a short philosophical text and reflecting on it in togetherness, using what we call "interpretive reading." This is a semi-contemplative procedure that allows participants to resonate with the text and with each other's ideas. After about 30 minutes, when participants had understood the text, we used a centering exercise of about 10 minutes to enter a contemplative state of mind. The heart of the session came next – a group contemplation of about one hour. Here we contemplated in togetherness from our inner depth on the ideas we found in the text, using various procedures and exercises. Following the contemplation, participants were invited to quietly connect the text to a personal experience, and in this way enrich both their understanding of the text and of themselves. The session ended with a short concluding exercise in which participants reflected on what had happened to them during the session.

It was not by coincidence that we chose this structure for our sessions. The sessions were especially designed to bring the participants to the right mental attitude. People usually need time to leave behind their busy everyday life and enter the contemplative mood. Simplicity of structure helps participants clear their minds from their many thoughts and images, focus themselves, and enter a steady state of mind. In a philosophical-contemplative retreat, it is important to respect the silence at every moment and to keep the mind in an inward-looking and self-reflective mode.

However, the right mental attitude is only one part of the philosophical-contemplative work. If you want your contemplation to be philosophical, then you must also bring philosophical ideas and issues into the process. For this reason, in each session we used one short philosophical text as our starting point, usually an excerpt of 1-2 pages from a longer philosophical work. The text helped us focus the session on one fundamental life-issue, and it enriched the discourse by offering philosophical ideas as material to work with.

Our sessions

In the first session, on Thursday morning, led by Ran, we used a passage from Henri Bergson's book

Time and Free Will. We chose to start with this specific text because it talks about an important element in philosophical contemplation, namely the depth of the self. According to Bergson, many ideas in our mind "float on the surface, like dead leaves on the water of a pond."[1] These ideas usually remain fixed and unchanged, as if they were external to our mind. Over time, they form a "thick crust" that produces much of our automatic, thoughtless behavior. When we let these external ideas guide us, we believe that we are acting freely, but in fact this is an illusion. Sometimes, however, a new movement in our depth revolts against this superficial crust, breaks through it and rises to the surface, in other words to our awareness.[2] As a result, we might act against what we previously considered the best rational choice, or we might experience a deep inner change in our perspective on life.

But why is this text important to us? Because an important aim of our philosophical-contemplative activity is to enable participants to go beyond their ordinary self, beyond the superficial level of ideas described by Bergson. What makes our practice different from ordinary philosophical discourse is that we do philosophy from our inner depth. We

---

1. Henri Bergson, *Time and Free Will*, Dover Publications, New York, 2001, page 135.
2. Ibid, pages 167-169.

reflect and communicate philosophically not just by using logical reasoning and analytic skills, but by thinking from a deep inner attitude.

The second day of the retreat dealt with another important topic in the group activity of philosophical contemplation: our relations to another person. As usual, the day was divided into a morning session and an afternoon session, each one consisting of a separate contemplative session. The two texts for the two sessions were taken from the Agora website (philopractice.org), which offers a large selection of brief philosophical text on a variety of everyday topics. The texts, by the philosophers Emmanuel Levinas and Martin Buber, were selected to offer two very different philosophical perspectives on the same topic.

In the morning session we used excerpts from Martin Buber's book *I and Thou*[3] which explains, in a poetic way, two kinds of relationships with others: I-You – a relationship of togetherness, and I-it – a distant, objectifying relationship. These relationships, according to Buber, are more basic than the self itself, since there is no such thing as a self that is not in relationship.

After reading the text several times in the procedure of "interpretive reading" and making sure

---

3. Martin Buber, *I and Thou*, Scriber, New York, 1970.

that everybody understood it, and after a centering exercise, we began with the contemplation itself. We chose several significant sentences, and the group repeated them again and again, one by one, in the practice *Ruminatio* which we borrowed from the monastic tradition. Here were some of the most powerful moments of the session. In this exercise, which might sometimes feel boring at first, participants fix their attention for a long time on the same sentence and the same concepts. This often produces a deep understanding, related to one's personal background. In order to deepen the experience, participants were instructed to connect in their mind the ideas with a personal experience, and then to express the result out loud in brief, condensed single sentences, in a procedure which we call "precious speaking." As a result, they found their personal understanding of themselves and of the ideas from the text deepened and enriched.

We concluded the session by sketching on a central sheet of paper what we call "a map of ideas." The sketch represented graphically the network of ideas we had contemplated, and it consolidated in the minds of participants the experience they have had. Before ending the session, participants shared with the group valuable moments which they had experienced during the session.

In the afternoon of the same day, Stefania Giordano led a session on a fragment from Emmanuel Levinas' essay "Ethics as a First philosophy." Levinas' view on the other person is very different from that of Buber, and it focuses on one's ethical responsibility to the other. "Before any particular expression, and under all particular expressions which cover and protect the Other with a face or expression, there is nakedness and destitution. In other words – extreme exposure defenselessness, vulnerability."[4]

Thus, while for Levinas my relation to another person is characterized by his vulnerability and my fundamental responsibility for him, this is not the case for Buber. We selected such different texts on purpose, in order to create a plurality of philosophical voices. In contemplation, we want to go beyond agreeing or disagreeing with a text. When we adopt a different philosophical perspective for the duration of the session, we experience a different way of looking at the world. Therefore, ideas from the history of philosophy help us gain a rich, polyphonic understanding of ourselves and our world.

---

4. Emmanuel Levinas, "Ethics as a First Philosophy," *The Levinas Reader*, Blackwell, Oxford, 1993, page 83. The quotation is a simplified version of Levinas' original text, which we used for the sake of accessibility.

During the rest of retreat, we continued to hold two sessions each day about a selected philosophical topic. On the following day, on Saturday, the topic was "love." We used texts by the Spanish thinker Miguel de Unamuno (from his *Tragic Sense of Life*) and the Russian philosopher Vladimir Solovyov (from his *The Meaning of Love*). While Unamuno understands love in terms of compassion for our mortality and our misery, Solovyov regards love as a way of overcoming our egotism and separateness towards integration with another human being, and with humanity in general.

On Sunday morning, the last full day of the retreat, we focused on the topic of thinking. In the morning I led a session on a text by Krishnamurti. For him, thinking separates us from the present because thought is always linked to the past. In the afternoon we reflected on a passage by the French philosopher Gabriel Marcel which characterizes the nature of profound ideas.

I should mention that during the retreat we also had two experimental sessions. In one of them Mike Roth, a participant from Germany, led the group in a contemplative walk, while reading a few paragraphs from *The Ego and Its Own* by the 19th century German philosopher Max Stirner. In the second experimental session, we split into small groups, and each of them dramatized a philosophical text. These experiments taught us that there are many ways in which a philosophical text can touch and enrich us.

The founding of the Deep Philosophy group

Sunday was the last day of the retreat, but we all knew that it was not a real end. We felt that something new had been being born. And this indeed was the case. On Monday morning, six of the participants still remained in Brando: The three organizers – Ran Lahav, Stefania Giordano, and myself, and three additional participants – Reginia Penner from Russia, Sebastian Drobny who is a German living in Austria, and Monika Obermeier from Germany. Sitting around the kitchen table, the idea came up that we should form a group devoted to developing this new kind of philosophy. We never stopped communicating since then.

The first retreat in Brando was the moment in which we first formulated the basic ideas of Deep Philosophy, but since then we have been working continuously to develop our ideas, our practices, our theoretical basis, and our connection with our roots in the history of philosophy. We have been giving additional retreats in Brando and elsewhere, presenting our approach in lectures and workshops, and offering online skype-sessions to interested people around the world. Although we find face-to-face activity more powerful, we put much emphasis on online sessions, because this format enables us to keep meeting regularly despite the geographic distances, and also to engage people around the world who want to join our activities.

In 2019 we felt ready to open our group to additional potential members. We started a program for "candidates" from several countries, which included both practical training and theory. Most of these candidates finished the program and became members of our group. Through the natural fluctuations which every group experiences, we have doubled the number of our members, and are in touch with a larger circle of people. We are not very eager to increase our membership and do not busy ourselves with marketing and publicity – we do not judge ourselves in terms of numbers, and we feel comfortable with our size. But the interest which people show in our activity strengthens our conviction that Deep Philosophy can be significant to many people who are looking to enrich and deepen their lives.

THE STRUCTURE OF A SESSION

Francesca D'Uva

The origin of Deep Philosophy is the human yearning for ultimate reality, a yearning that is experienced by everyone, whether more consciously or less consciously. And when we seek realness, we sometime gain access to it, at least for a few moments.

It might seem that this search belongs to the area of philosophy, because philosophy's task is to explore reality, but this is inaccurate. Philosophical discussions are often discursive and analytic, which is not enough to satisfy our yearning. Discursive philosophy can only think "about" reality and inspect it from a distance like an external observer. It cannot help us get in touch with it or embody it. In contrast, in Deep Philosophy we seek to bridge the distance between theory and reality, and reconnect with our reality by getting in touch with our inner depth. We do this primarily by resonating with the "voices" of humanity that express themselves in human thought. This is a path of self-transformation which opens in us a new dimension of understanding life from our inner depths.

In this path we typically use philosophical texts from the Western tradition. A philosophical text can be seen as a translation of the dimension of depth into certain universal ideas, and these ideas have the power to resonate in the depth of our being and trigger a process of self-transformation.

Our attitude to a philosophical text is contemplative. Through contemplation we guide our mind to go beyond the words of the text, into a deeper dimension from which the words themselves originate. Therefore, while reading the text we do not try to analyze or criticize it, but rather to resonate with the voices of the text, as well as with the voices of our fellow contemplators, in a polyphonic and contemplative dialogue that takes place within the group.

A philosophical-contemplative session, whether online or face-to-face, is our tool to achieve this goal. But in order for the session to take us towards this goal, it has to be structured and managed appropriately. In this article I will discuss the formats of philosophical-contemplative sessions which we have developed in Deep Philosophy.

The general parameters of a session

A Deep Philosophy session is normally led by a group-member who serves as the facilitator and makes sure that the session would flow appropriately. The group usually consists of three to twelve participants, and the session lasts about ninety minutes. Sessions may be held online or face-to-face. Online sessions are usually conducted through the Skype platform and with the help of the Google Docs interface which provides a common space for writing. Face-to-face sessions are typically conducted in one-time meetings or in philosophical retreats, like the ones that are periodically organized by the Deep Philosophy Group. In all of these modes, a similar structure is followed. While the sense of intimacy among group-members may be greater in face-to-face meeting, the outcome is the same.

The facilitator's first task is to select a philosophical text on which the group will contemplate. The text is carefully chosen. It must be rich enough to lend itself to contemplation, and it must contain within itself the imprints of the depth which Deep Philosophy seeks scattered among the philosophical words. Especially useful are philosophical texts that deal with self-transformation, because they express the understanding of the split between the superficial dimension of our life and our deeper dimension which embodies our realness. The superficial dimension is the one we experience in our everyday life, while the deeper one appears only in special moments that are usually brief yet significant, which is what Deep Philosophy seeks to create.

The facilitator accompanies the group through the contemplation of the text in a structured yet flexible path. Each text can be used in several different ways, thus producing different emphases, interactions, and resonance effects. The facilitator, the group, and the text create together the philosophical space within which the door opens to the participants' inner depth and inner realness.

The skeleton of a session

Although sessions are flexible, in general they have a similar skeleton: a centering exercise, an exercise for understanding of the text, contemplative activity, a quiet exercise, closure, and meta-conversation.

A session typically starts with a short centering exercise, directed by the facilitator. Its role is to separate between the busy flow of daily life and the tranquil, almost-sacred space that is required for philosophical contemplation. It usually lasts no more than five minutes. Participants are asked to sit comfortably and close their eyes. The facilitator's voice will do the rest, guiding the participants to focus on their breath, body parts, or some imagined scene.

In the next step, participants focus on the philosophical text which had been selected by the facilitator. But before contemplating, they must first understand the ideas in text. This is often done in the semi-contemplative exercise of "interpretive reading" in which participants read the text section by section, each section several times, while adding their own brief interpretations. In this way they broaden and enrich the meanings they discern in the text. At the same time, the repeated reading of each passage creates a sense of chanting, and therefore the beginning of a contemplative atmosphere. This exercise usually lasts about thirty to forty minutes. If the text is difficult and requires further clarification, the facilitator might add an exercise of "map of ideas" in which participants chart graphically the main concepts of the text and their interrelations.

Now that the text is clear and the mind is quiet and focused, it is time to delve into the contemplative part of the session, which usually takes about half an hour. Often the facilitator starts with a few rounds of the contemplative exercise called "Ruminatio" – a repeated reading of a selected sentence over and over again like a "mantra." Another contemplative exercise, which can be given after the Ruminatio, is "precious speaking." Here the facilitator asks the participants to complete a sentence in so-called precious speaking – carefully selected and articulated words without redundancy – while resonating with the text and with each other. The repetition, the resonation, and the carefully selected words create a sense of intense inner listening. This often gives birth to deep insights.

Following the contemplative phase, the group continues with a quite exercise designed to translate into words the deep insights which each participant has experienced. This can be done in one of several exercises, for example by instructing each one to write a couple of poetic verses and then combining them into one group poem. This allows the participants to share with the group their experiences and insights while creating a polyphony of voices. In a philosophical retreat, this stage can be followed by a quiet activity together such as a quiet philosophical walk or drawing. This provides each participant an individual space of inner reflection and solitude. It may be followed by a few moment of sharing of experiences and thoughts.

The session has thus come to an end. To summarize and integrate the session, the facilitator asks each participant to share freely what they are taking with them from the session. Participants may share general impressions, ideas and insights, or experiences that had surfaced in their minds during the contemplation.

The facilitator now declares that the session has ended, but he may still invite the participants to step out of the session and think ABOUT it. This so-called meta-conversation has a double purpose: to provide the facilitator with valuable feedback, and to help the Deep Philosophy group to think about future development of its activities.

Overall, the different stages of a session should flow one into the next seamlessly, with no interruptions between one activity and another. In a good session, each element is exactly where it should be, distinct yet joining the others into an overall whole.

Different forms of sessions

In our Deep Philosophy group we have developed several different kinds of sessions, each one focused on a different goal and accordingly having a somewhat different structure. These include sessions focused on contemplation, sessions focused on understanding the text, sessions focused on sharing personal experiences, and voicing sessions. Although each of these contains the same basic elements – contemplation, understanding, and sharing personal experiences – nevertheless each kind emphasizes one element more than others.

a. *Understanding-oriented sessions*: This kind of session aims at clarifying the selected text and exploring its basic ideas. Although this requires some degree of analytic thinking, the group still maintains a semi-contemplative state of mind. A large part of the session is devoted to semi-contemplative exercises that focus on the conceptual landscape of the text.

The session usually begins (possibly after the centering exercise) with a round of text reading and so-called "interpretive reading." As explained earlier, interpretive reading is an exercise in which participants go through the text section after section, each participant reading one section at a time, while adding his own brief interpretations. In this way, the participants come to understand the surface meaning of the text. They are now ready to delve into the text more deeply to understand in greater detail the text's conceptual landscape.

To do so, the facilitator selects several key concepts or phrases, and invites the participants to reflect on them, using one or more exercises designed for this purpose. For example, the exercise of "Ruminatio" mentioned before (repeating a selected sentence over and over again in a chant-like repetition) helps create a contemplative state of mind that is attentive to hidden meanings. In another exercise, participants resonate with a passage from the text by uttering sentences in "precious speaking"–

brief condensed sentences in which each word is treated as precious and is carefully selected. Alternatively, the facilitator may offer unfinished sentences which the participants have to finish spontaneously in precious speaking, thus giving voice their personal understanding of the text. Still another possibility is the "as opposed to what" exercise in which participants construct sentences that are opposed to the text. This helps to clarify the text's viewpoint by way of contrasting it with alternative ways of approaching the issue.

An understanding-oriented session typically ends with a final round in which participants are invited to share which sentence or phrase has intrigued them and "invited" them to think deeply – in other words, served them as what we call "a door to the depth."

b. *Contemplation-oriented sessions*: The goal of a contemplation-oriented session is to create a deep and powerful contemplative experience of one's inner depth while listening inwardly to deep insights. Much of the activity in such sessions is therefore devoted to contemplative exercises that employ silent contemplation and inner attention.

The session can begin with a centering exercise to create inner focus and silence. This is usually followed by several rounds of Ruminatio (repetitive reading of a selected sentence in a chant-like fashion) or a sentence-completion exercise in precious speaking (condensed brief sentences). The emphasis here is not on trying to understand the details of the text, but on inner listening to how the text speaks within us. For this reason, participants are instructed to think and speak "from" the text and not "about" it. Sometimes the group is given a few quiet minutes to read portions of the text gently and very slowly in what is called "gentle reading." The resulting atmosphere is particularly silent and absorbed.

To conclude the session, the facilitator asks the participants to reflect on the session as a whole, to recall the insights which they had received during the session, and share them in precious speaking. The facilitator may also use a poem-writing exercise, since poetical thinking helps the mind to listen silently to the sound of the words and their precise meaning, and thus to listen to one's inner depth. Here the exercise "group poem" can be used: Each participant gives voice to his insights by writing two poetic verses. The group's two-verse pieces are then combined together into one group-poem, and group-members read it together and resonate with it in a personal way. Through the many voices and experiences the group becomes one in poetry.

c. *Sessions oriented to personal experience*: The goal of these sessions is to connect our contemplative experiences to our everyday life, in order not to keep our deep insights isolated from our daily activity but rather let them enrich and deepen it. Therefore, in this kind of session participants recall relevant everyday moments and relate them to the deep insights that emerged from the text.

The session usually begins with the usual centering exercise and interpretive reading of the text. This may be followed by several rounds of precious speaking (brief condensed sentences) on some of the main concepts or phrases suggested by the facilitator, as well as Ruminatio (chant-like repetition) of relevant sentences. The facilitator then asks participants to recall a personal experience that resonates with the text. The experience does not have to be dramatic or special – on the contrary, small everyday experiences are preferable.

After a few seconds of silent reflection, they are invited to share the experiences they remember in brief and carefully-selected words. Importantly, they are asked not to talk "about" their experience ("I remember that I was amazed...") and not to describe it in detail, but rather to talk "from" the experience, as if the words are emerging from the experience while it is happening ("I can see him looking at me, and I feel amazed..."). Once an experience has been shared, the other participants are asked to enter the experiencer's world and imagine themselves in the experiencer's position. They resonate with the experience in precious speaking as if it was their own experience. Their aim is to enrich the original experience by adding to it additional details, meanings and qualities.

To conclude the session, the facilitator may use some poem-writing exercise, since poetical thinking helps the mind listen silently to our inner depth. For this purpose, the exercise "group poem" can be used (each participant writes two poetic verses, and the verses are then combined into one longer poem). Alternatively, a round of sharing what each participant is taking from the session can also be used.

d. *Voicing sessions*: The goal of voicing sessions is to help participants find a deep insight within themselves, develop it fully, and give voice to it. The session starts, like other kinds of session, with a centering exercise and interpretive reading of the text. A few rounds of Ruminatio may follow, as well as sentence-completion in precious speaking.

The next step is the heart of the session. Here participants remain in silence for several minutes and gently let their mind hover over the words of the text. They listen inwardly to the meanings and insights that may arise in their consciousness, and follow them as they develop. Gentle writing – writing on a sheet of paper carefully, slowly, and nicely – may also be used. While reading and writing gently, they maintain inner quiet, relax the control of the thinking mind, and resist its tendency to impose its own opinions and interpretations. They savor the words, notice phrases that attract their attention, and listen to what those phrases "want" to tell them.

Several times during the session, participants share with each other some of their insights, but in minimal speaking. They do not attempt to give a full account of what happened to them, but only a partial glimpse of their inner experience. To end the session, participants are invited to share a glimpse of their experiences during the session. Since the atmosphere is very contemplative and silent, it is best to end the session with minimal speaking.

Conclusion

I have described here in broad outlines the normal structure of Deep Philosophy sessions. Obviously, there are many possible variation, mixtures, personal styles, as well as additional elements that may be added, but these are beyond the scope of this paper. I should emphasize that my account is by no means final. Deep Philosophy is continuously developing, and new exercises and formats are born every once in a while. Indeed, we see ourselves as seekers, always on the way, never possessing a final doctrine. The ongoing process of exploring and discovering is an essential part of what Deep Philosophy is.

Furthermore, we recognize and cherish individual differences. Each one of us is a unique individual who encounters a given text or session from the perspective of unique life-experiences. The polyphonic richness of the many voices of humanity is a valuable treasure which should not be suppressed in the name of some unified dogma. Therefore, unlike disciplines such as yoga or martial arts, we do not seek to impose on our practitioners one "correct" way of practicing. Our ideas and methods are always only starting points for a personal journey of exploration. And this journey becomes rich and meaningful when we restrain our tendency to quickly judge and evaluate, let ourselves be carried along by the group's polyphonic dynamics, experience our philosophical togetherness, and let it all gently sink into the depths of our being.

PROCEDURES FOR STUDYING TEXTS

Massimiliano Bavieri

Using philosophical texts in Deep Philosophy

Our goal in a Deep Philosophy session is to contemplate on philosophical ideas from our inner depth, and thus let new understandings emerge from a deeper dimension of our being. The problem is that it is very difficult for contemplators to compose insightful ideas on the spot, out of nothing, within a few minutes. Therefore, in each contemplative session we usually work with a philosophical text, selected from the history of philosophy, to serve us as a starting point. Although a philosophical text usually expresses a specific opinion, the contemplators are not asked to agree with it. The text only provides the materials on which we work, the ideas to develop or modify or replace, the images and distinctions and concepts which we might want to use in our personal way.

In addition, a philosophical text also helps the group focus its attention on a common topic and a common perspective (for example, a certain perspective on authenticity, or on death, beauty, love), and thus create a common language for communication. Furthermore, the text also serves to take us beyond our usual everyday thoughts to new unexplored perspectives on life.

A Deep Philosophy session is usually divided into two parts: first, understanding our selected text, and second, going beyond it. In the first part, we read the text together in order to understand its basic ideas. To do so, we often "resonate" with passages from the text by rephrasing them or adding to them a few words of our own. In the second part, we go beyond the text by contemplating on its ideas and developing them in our own personal way. Here, we can use the practice of "voicing," in which we express our own personal voice from our inner depth, beyond the voice of the text.

Starting a contemplative session with the study of a text presents a special challenge: How to conduct this study in a way that would not involve too much rational and analytic thinking. On the one hand, we want to understand what the text says in a clear and organized way. But on the other hand, we want to prepare our minds for the contemplative thinking of the second part of the session. We don't want to orient our minds to an "academic" way of thinking, which would be inconsistent with contemplation. A lecture or a discussion would obviously not be a suitable method of studying the text. What is needed is a semi-contemplative technique which would be systematic enough for understanding, but open and fluid enough to prepare us for contemplation.

The procedure of Interpretive Reading

There are two main semi-contemplative techniques for studying a text which we have developed in our Deep Philosophy group: "interpretive reading" and "map of ideas." Let us start with the first one.

Interpretive reading is often conducted at the beginning of the session (possibly after a brief centering exercise). Each participant in his or her turn reads a few sentences from the text – but not exactly word for word. Instead, readers add a few words of their own, whenever they deem it appropriate, by way of explaining the intention of the text, rephrasing, sharpening, offering a synonym of a difficult word or a simplified paraphrase of a complicated sentence, etc. The result is that each reader says a few sentences that are similar to the original but are also different, corresponding to the text but also more elaborate.

After the first reader (usually the facilitator) finishes reading, the next participant reads the same section from the text, but with his or her own interpretation. In this way the same section is read in the circle again and again several times, as many times as determined by the facilitator, depending on the difficulty of the text and the available time. The repetition of similar phrases over and over again creates a sense of chanting, which contributes to the contemplative atmosphere.

Several guidelines are important here in order to maintain a semi-contemplative atmosphere. First, readers are instructed to limit their interpretation to no more than a few words and avoid long speeches. Second, readers should not speak *about* the text but *with* the text, as if speaking from the text's perspective. This means that they should not express judgment, agreement or disagreement, or personal opinions. Such comments originate from our discursive patterns of thinking, which are opposed to our contemplative attitude. They must be pushed aside, so that the deeper dimension within us would find the space to express itself.

The result of this technique is a group-reflection on the text which is semi-discursive or semi-rational. It helps the participants understand the main ideas, but it also starts putting their minds in a state of resonating with the text, just as one physical objet begins to resonate when it enters into sympathy with another object that is vibrating. Still, this way of speaking is not yet fully contemplative, since it involves elements of discursive thinking, or thinking-about. It is much more discursive than the later stage of contemplation, when we limit our speech to what we call "precious speaking" – brief, poetic phrases expressed from our inner depth, without direct references to the text, without redundancy or repetition, so that each word is precise and precious like a gem, or like a gift to the group.

Why don't we want the reader to make personal judgments about the text? The answer, already given in part, is that when I express personal judgment about something, I "speak about" it while inspecting it from the outside. "Speaking about" involves a relationship between a subject (the "I" who thinks and speaks) and the described object, thus transforming me into an observer who is external to what I am speaking about.

Some degree of speaking-about or thinking-about is necessary at this early stage of the session, since we want to understand what the text says. But in as far as possible, the speaking must also be a "speaking from," that is, giving voice to one's subjectivity. While reading and commenting on the text, the reader must therefore enter the text personally, in the first person, and strive to speak through the particular voice of the writer of the text, as if expressing the reader's point of view.

Moreover, during the interpretive process, it sometimes happens that we are touched by the interpretations of one or more previous readers. Even in this case, however, we don't express agreement and we don't comment on what they had said. Instead, we resonate with their interpretations by repeating their words or rephrasing them or elaborating on them. This means that we can resonate not only with the text, but also with the words of our companions. In short, in the interpretive reading procedure, we judge neither the text nor what others say, but only resonate with them like different voices in a choir.

The metaphor of "resonating with," taken from the world of music, is rich and instructive. Singers or musicians, too, when performing a piece, resonate with the original musical score, as well as with other performers. Each of them plays or sings in a unique and personal way, even though the musical score is the same. This is why experienced listeners can identify performers by their style. If, for example, we know the interpretive style of the greatest international pianists, we might identify successfully which pianist is now playing the music to which we are listening. Moreover, the performance of a given musician is usually influenced by the interpretations of previous musicians. Here too we find a parallel between music and the interpretive reading procedure, where readers can resonate with those who had read and interpreted the text before them.

The procedure of Map of Ideas

Another procedure of studying a text at the beginning of a session is based on mapping out on paper the text's central concepts. The central concepts of a text can be seen as a "landscape," where each concept occupies a particular place within the whole. This is analogous to a geographical landscape, only each "landmark" is a concept instead of a mountain, lake, road, etc. If we map out on paper the "conceptual landscape" of the text, we would understand its basic structure.

To start this procedure, participants read the text out loud, one after the other, paragraph by paragraph. In this way the group may read each paragraph three or four times, and the repeated reading creates a sense of chanting. After the entire text has been read, participants are asked to identify the central concepts contained in the text, and they do so by simply stating them out loud. In order to maintain a semi-contemplative atmosphere, they do not explain their choice, limiting their speaking to two or three words.

For example, if the text in question is from Plato's Allegory of the Cave, participants might call out: "prison," "shadows," "illusion," "reality," and so on.

As the calling out of concepts continues, the facilitator writes them down for everybody to see. In online meetings, this can be done on a real-time writing tool such as Google Doc. If the meeting is face-to-face, concepts can be written in the middle of the circle on a sheet of paper, or each concept on a small piece of paper.

After sufficient concepts have been mentioned, it is now time to arrange them in a way that would represent the structure of the text. For example, if the text revolves around a dichotomy between two concepts (truth and falsity, subject and object, etc.), then these two concepts are placed in the middle. Relations between concepts can be indicated by lines or other symbols. The result is a map of the conceptual landscape of the text as if observed from the top of a mountain.

This exercise helps the group visualize the conceptual structure of the text. It also helps participants, even more than in the interpretive reading procedure, to place themselves inside the world of the text and view it from the perspective of its author. They become witnesses of the ideas of the text, as if they had created them themselves and are living in them personally. Unlike interpretive reading, however, this procedure does not include going beyond the text and responding to it with one's own ideas. If desired, this can be done in a separate procedure afterwards.

Awakening a personal mode of understanding

The result of those two procedures, interpretive reading and map of ideas, is that we achieve a special kind of understanding of the text, different from the theoretical understanding we obtain through ordinary academic studies. Although this personal understanding may lack the scientific rigor that is the goal of academic reading, it involves deeper aspects of our self which lie beyond abstract reasoning.

Resonating personally with the text – and to a lesser extent with other readers – plays a central role in interpretive reading. It helps us push aside our normal thinking patterns, which are limited to our automatic psychological structures and are disconnected from deeper aspects of our being. What comes to the surface, and what enters into personal resonance with the text, is what I am beyond my usual opinions about people, about the world, about life. These opinions tend to dominate our mind, leaving no room for anything else and repressing our inner depth.

The procedures of interpretive reading and map of ideas therefore serve to immerse us in the philosophical text and help us enter its conceptual network, while going beyond our normal psychological self which lives on the surface of our being. They allow us to explore philosophical ideas from within, so that we can assume, to some extent, the point of view of the author. They thus enable us to personally appropriate the text, as if it was our own creation, as a voice expressing the reader's point of view.

This is why it is important that we avoid inspecting the philosophical text from an objective external perspective, and instead we delve into it and place ourselves in the world it presents. This helps us to break down the resistance of our normal limited self to change its usual ways of understanding the basic aspects of life, such as love, death, friendship, and virtue. Thus, a new dimension of understanding opens up for us, beyond our everyday thinking patterns which have gradually crystalized a rigid system of opinions, which might be too narrow for experiencing and understanding what is really real.

The transformative text

The philosophers we choose to read in our Deep Philosophy session are often those we call "transformative philosophers," because they call readers to change their attitude to life. Their texts realize what Kierkegaard calls "existential communication," which is a mode of speaking and writing that encourages readers to abandon their inauthentic attitudes, or at least reduce them, in order to open space for a deeper reality to express itself, including one's fundamental attitude to life and reality. This type of communication is opposed to objectifying communication, which deals only with what is describable and measurable.

Existential communication engages two dimensions of the human being: the visible and ephemeral surface of our life, and our hidden possibilities of living which tend to escape our notice. Existential communication moves from one individual to another individual, from philosopher to reader. The communicator engages the reader or listener directly, calling him to follow his duty to take on the task of transformation, which the author himself has personally taken upon himself. The reader is encouraged to renew a full relationship with his truest self, which is hidden from sight by the petrified layers of his being. The transformative philosophical text serves, therefore, as a voice that encourages the individual to explore and discover new possibilities of existence that go beyond one's accustomed way of living.

Such philosophical texts, when used in the Deep Philosophy sessions, serve as "doors to the depth" of existence. In other words, they make the reader aware that he has not yet taken the path of transcending his habitual and superficial life, but that he has the possibility and the duty to do so.

The procedures of interpretive reading and map of ideas are designed to invite the reader to take a first step through the "entrance door" that leads to the path of transformation, represented by the transformative philosophical text.

PERSPECTIVES ON INNER DEPTH [5]

Kirill Rezvushkin

Inner depth is a central concept in Deep Philosophy, and the experience of inner depth is central for our group. What does inner depth mean? I suggest that it is best to understand it not in terms of one unitary definition, but as a meeting point of several different complimentary perspectives. In this chapter I will explain some of the perspectives that have made this concept rich and meaningful for me.

The personal autobiographical perspective

How did I become interested in Deep Philosophy, and thus with inner depth? After studying at university philology and history, I started to develop my own philosophical worldview. I was not satisfied with the humanities and with ordinary philosophical discussions because they were far from life, and they forced me to abandon myself. I felt that my life was going in the wrong direction and I suffered from isolation. I tried psychoanalysis and existential

---

5. This article was prepared as part of the RFBR project No. 17-33-00021, "Theory and Practice of Philosophical Counseling: Comparative Approach."

psychology, and this brought to some tangible results, but something was still wrong. Something I could not recognize was knocking on the door of my mind. My life was not as authentic as I wanted it to be.

And then I heard from my professor Sergey Borisov about the international movement of philosophical practice, which is based on the idea that philosophy can make our life fuller. In 2016, my philosophy department sent me, together with my good friends and colleagues Regina Penner and Artyr Dydrov, to participate in a seminar of philosophical practice in France. I was impressed with the critical thinking approach of philosophical practice, but during the seminar I also experienced a traumatic inner conflict. As a result, I was overwhelmed by my unresolved inner difficulties, and out of frustration I pushed them out of my mind.

Finally, I decided to cautiously try a gentler approach to philosophical practice. In April 2017, my colleague Sergey Borisov invited Ran Lahav to my university in Russia to give sessions of philosophical companionship to the academic philosophical audience. The sessions touched me and inspired me. Later, in June of the same year, I took part in several online sessions, facilitated by Ran, with the participation of Michele Zese and Elisabeth Biber, two philosophical practitioners from

Italy and Austria. As a result, my attitude to philosophy changed dramatically. I came to the conclusion that philosophy could help me make my inner life more coherent and focused. I was surprised to realize that not only psychology and religion can transform people.

At the beginning of September 2017, Regina participated in the first philosophical retreat in Brando, Italy, where the Deep Philosophy Group was founded. I was still hesitating, even after she came back and shared with us her powerful experiences. I made up my mind only after I myself experienced the transformative potential of philosophy, during a retreat that was given by Ran in his second visit in Russia in November of 2017. From this retreat I still carry with me many precious memories, for example a philosophical meditative walk on the shore of a lake in which I felt unity with the entire world. Soon afterwards, I received an invitation to join the Deep Philosophy group and to participate in the second retreat of Deep Philosophy in Brando, in February of 2018. I accepted with great pleasure.

The perspective of our group activity

Although inner depth is a central concept in our Deep Philosophy group, we do not try to impose on all of us one single definition of this concept. We share a broad, general understanding of it, but each one of us has his or her specific version of it. These personal differences help inspire us, and they create a polyphony in which we are united and yet remain ourselves.

One might wonder why the search for our inner depth is important. Most of us would answer that in everyday life our behavior tends to be automatic, and this results in meaninglessness and inauthenticity, even if we do not suffer from any specific personal problem. To make our life more authentic and meaningful, we should gain access to an inner dimension within us that is a source of vitality, and try to remain connected with it on a regular basis.

Sessions of philosophical companionship create a sense of togetherness, and the interaction between us is very different from cold academic discussions. Contemplation in togetherness takes us beyond our individual psychology and helps us reach our inner depth. In ordinary life, this is not easy to achieve, because we are distant from ourselves and from our vitality. This distance from life can also happen in academic philosophy, when vital philosophical discourse that is rooted in human existence is substituted for abstract doctrines. It is well known that philosophical activity at university are usually far from the "spiritual exercises"[6] of ancient philosophers, as described by Pierre Hadot.

In Deep Philosophy, philosophizing together from our inner depth helps restore our sense of authenticity and fullness of life.

The perspectives of philosophical theories

Several theories from the field of philosophy offer interesting interpretations of the notion of inner depth. One such theory is Paul Tillich's theory of "symbols" in his book *Dynamics of Faith*.[7] Tillich defines a symbol as an object – a text, a poem, a painting, a ritual, etc. – that points beyond itself, opening us to a dimension of reality which is otherwise inaccessible to us, and opening that reality to us. This suggests that an appropriate symbol can help connect us to a hidden reality within us – our inner depth – and transform us in important ways.

We may say, using Tillich's terminology, that the texts which we use in our Deep Philosophy sessions function as "symbols." These are specially selected fragments, taken from philosophical books or essays, often a little bit simplified for the ease of reading. The texts themselves are usually regarded as abstract

---

6. Pierre Hadot, *Philosophy as a Way of Life*, Blackwell, Oxford, 1995.
7. Paul Tillich, *Dynamics of Faith*, Harper&Row, New York, 1956, Chapter 3, section 1: "The meaning of symbol."

academic theories. But when we read them in our group with the help of special procedures, we come to relate to them differently, from a contemplative state of mind, and in togetherness with others. This allows us to go beyond our normal psychological structures and get in touch with hidden dimensions of our being, or what we call our inner depth.

The powerful sense of inner connectedness and awakening which we feel during the session can extend beyond the session. This indeed is what happened to me during the second Brando retreat, in an experience which I cannot forget. After taking part in so many powerful contemplative sessions, I discovered that my state of mind had altered. When I went out with my friends for a walk in the woods, the path now seemed completely unfamiliar as if I was seeing it for the first time. I admired the beautiful winter landscape and the snow covering the trees, but to the amazement of my friends, I did not fully recognize the place. My perception was as fresh as it had never been before, and my life felt rich and full. Sadly, some time afterwards my old patterns returned. Yet, my mind had shifted in an irreversible way.

We can also understand this inner transformation from a somewhat different perspective, using the ideas of the British thinker Owen Barfield. In his book *Poetic Diction*,[8] he argues that poetic metaphors can reveal to us the holistic network of meanings in our world, before they are dissected and fragmented by our rational mind. And indeed, poetic writing is sometimes used in our group to attain a different way of thinking and comprehending. For example, in one of the procedures we sometimes use at the end of a session, we compose together a group-poem. The poem is made of the individual verses which each participant has written from personal experiences during the session. The process arouses in us a poetic state of mind, helping us to look at the topic of the session in a different, deeper and more authentic way.

Overall, we might say that in our sessions, three elements are especially important in enabling the experience of inner depth: The contemplative activity, the text, and the sense of togetherness with our companions.

Metaphors of inner depth

It is not easy to think about inner depth in a rational, analytic way. Metaphors offer us a more accessible and immediate perspective, and indeed they sometimes touch me meaningfully.

---

8. Owen Barfield, *Poetic Diction*, Wesleyan University Press, Middletown CT, 1973.

One example is the image of light, which came up during the second Brando retreat as a metaphor for inner depth. The metaphor reminds me of a page on the Agora website that deals with philosophies of inner truth.[9] An amusing photo appears on that page, its caption stating that a refrigerator too has inner light. In my opinion, this is not just a joke – it is also a nice metaphor worth examining carefully.

The light inside a refrigerator turns on when we open the door, and it turns off when the door is closed. The effort to close the door is significantly smaller than the effort to open it. In an analogous way, it is more difficult to attain (to "turn on") our inner depth than to lose it. Moreover, usually the refrigerator's light turns on only for short periods of time, after a conscious action on our part to open the door – analogous to the effort needed to reach our inner depth. Still, the refrigerator's light may fail to turn on because of a malfunction or a burned light bulb; it will turn on only if everything is functional, just like in the case of our soul.

Another metaphor that touches me comes from Marcus Aurelius' statement that "it is in your power to retire into yourself whenever you choose."[10] To me this sounds as if my inner depth is my favorite

---

9. https://philopractice.org/web/inner-truth-2017
10. Marcus Aurelius, *Meditations*, Prometheus Books, Amherst NY, 1991, Book IV 3.

couch where I can always rest. My inner depth is a basis, a ground, a foundation on which I can rely.

A third example comes from a dream I had not long ago, which might be considered as a metaphor for my current situation. In the dream I saw a stray dog walking down the street. Its coat had been originally white, but now it was covered with dark filth. I understood this to mean that the happiness you achieve by reaching your depth is never pure. When we reach depth, we experience a strong existential feeling of authenticity, accompanied by a sense of happiness. But complete happiness is a rare ideal, since in real life it is usually marred by interruptions. Usually we have some poison in the honey. Therefore, the dog's white covered by black may be seen as a metaphor for the inevitable dialectics of good and bad.

Interestingly, the refrigerator metaphor and the stray dog metaphor have something in common. A refrigerator may contain plenty of food, in contrast to a stray dog who is hungry and "empty." Therefore, the first image seems connected with a sense of fullness, and therefore with inner depth, while the second image seems connected with a sense of lack and emptiness. In both cases, happiness appears as something that calls me to reach it. Its voice is sometimes strong, but sometimes, in the routine of everyday life, it is weak.

Personally, such metaphors help me to think about the inner depth and connect with it.

The religious and psychological perspectives

The topic of inner depth is also discussed in psychology and in religion, and these perspectives must not be ignored. We can see the relation between Deep Philosophy, psychology and religion, with the help of a fable by the famous Russian writer Ivan Krylov, called "The Swan, The Pike and the Crab."[11]

One day a swan, a pike (a deep-water fish), and a crab tried to pull a loaded cart together. The swan pulled it upwards, the pike pulled it into the sea, and the crab pulled it backwards. Obviously, they tried to achieve the same goal, but each in its own conflicting way. "It is not for us to say who is right," Krylov wisely notes in his fable. This conflict can be viewed as a symbol of the three disciplines: The swan which floats on the surface of the water can symbolize the psychologist who works with the visible "surface" of everyday patterns. The crab which pulls backwards can be related to religion, which tells you that in order to save your soul you must pull back from common behaviors. The pike which lives in the depth of the sea symbolizes for me deep philosophers.

---

11. "The Swan, The Pike and the Crab," Ivan Krylov, *The Frogs Who Begged for a Tsar: (and 61 other Russian fables)*, Russian Information Services, Montpelier VT, 2010, Chapter 25.

In the depth, we can find treasures of our experience that are hidden from us. But deep on the ocean floor we can also find far less pretty creatures, such as anglerfish which look as if they came from a nightmare. This refers to traumatic experiences we can discover by exploring our depth. Of course, such an exploration is a psychological matter, but after we resolve the hidden traumatic experiences, we can continue to examine the depth by means of Deep Philosophy.

In our depth we can also find our inner voice, like Socrates' daemon. From a psychological or psychoanalytical perspective, this inner voice can be understood as the super-ego or the collective unconscious. But my own inner experience tells me that these interpretations are one-sided, and they do not grasp the fullness of the experience.

Religious interpretations, too, can be narrowing, when they are used to fit an experience into the framework of one specific tradition. But this is not necessarily the case. As I noted earlier, Tillich's theological conception of symbols is closely related to what we do in our Deep Philosophy group, even though it emerges from his specific Protestant tradition. Furthermore, the religious perspective can sometimes enrich the philosophical activity. For example, I remember that Ran once suggested, in an online session with me and Michele, that "in our ensembles we should find a way to acknowledge the understandings we receive, in order to make them more meaningful and inspiring." He then e-mailed us an ancient Gnostic thanksgiving prayer which gives thanks to God for an insight received: "*We give thanks to You! Every soul and heart is lifted up to You… We rejoice, having been illuminated by Your knowledge…*"[12]

When I read this text, it struck me that a prayer can be seen as a channel of communication that connects me to the divine, or to the ultimate You as Martin Buber would say. This suggested to me that inner depth is a You – somebody I can relate to personally (although it is also more than a You). This demonstrates how the religious perspective enriched my philosophical experience.

Depth and the sense of truth and realness

We strive to reach our inner depth, which is the only place from which we can philosophize truly. The various procedures of Deep Philosophy help us gain access to our inner depth, and once we are connected to it, we can speak from it in togetherness with others. We seek ways to find our inner depth in order to elevate ourselves throughout everyday life.

---

12. "The Prayer of Thanksgiving" James Robinson, *The Nag Hammadi Library*, HarperCollins, New York, 1988, page 329.

I experience my inner depth as my inner truth. I experience it as an inner light, an inner silence, an answer to my distress, a consolation. If you taste it once, you would not be able to refuse it later.

While in my depth, I do not think in a linear way through time, but like a timeless chain of still frames. Yet, despite the absence of the dimension of time, inner speech takes place in it. I may hear an inner voice speaking in me, sometimes responding to my questions, sometimes before any question arises. It may bring consolation, or it may provide an I-You dialogue. Of course, when I speak about inner questions and answers I do not mean that the inner depth should be viewed as an encyclopedia or catechism.

At the same time, inner depth also has a historical dimension, and while in it, I feel connected with tradition. In this sense, I experience togetherness not only "horizontally" with my companions who are flesh and blood in the philosophical sessions, but also "vertically" with people from the past.

An example is our retreat house in Brando, which belongs to our generous host Michele Zese, and which inspired me and stimulated my imagination. It was built in medieval times – its old oven for chestnuts can still be found in the forest nearby, and then rebuilt in modern times. In the contemplative atmosphere of the retreat I kept in mind the continuity of the place through history. After participating in many sessions, experiencing real togetherness, and concentrating intensely on reaching my inner depth, I finally succeeded to "enter" the past. I was no longer looking at the past from the outside but feeling immersed in it. I felt as if I was myself a medieval artisan who had dedicated his talents to serving God, sitting in his medieval workshop and squinting at the sun. Through this imagery I felt the divine light of ultimate reality, and this filled me with a yearning to create something great and worthy of offering to God.

Long-term impact

To sum up, the experience of inner depth is not one thing. It is the meeting point of a wide range of perspectives, including one's personal history, togetherness with companions, philosophical theories, metaphors and images, ideas from religion and psychology, the sense of reality and time. Personally for me, those perspectives, as I described them here, gave my experience of depth its incredible richness and power.

The experience of inner depth had a long-term impact. It has given me a clearer focus on what is happening not only inside me, but in reality in general, so I can speak from it and describe it, without judging it. This allows me to expand myself, gently and openly, with complete acceptance. It also allows me to see what is of real value – ultimate value, beyond all appearances – and put aside what had only seemed valuable. With my companions I have unlocked a precious dimension, discovering in it new treasures and sharing them with each other. As a result, I now feel greater freedom and inspiration, and I am able to do what I truly want beyond some of my old psychological patterns which tend to influence my actions and choices. These changes seem like a tectonic shift within me, and they help satisfy my yearning for a sense of realness.

At the time of my experience of inner depth, I let my inner depth lead me, knowing that I needed to die in it to become my true self – not for eternity but for a moment, so that later I could remember this precious experience for a long time. After all, the experience itself cannot go on forever. At some point I had to succumb to the laws that govern my body and psychology, and return to my usual limited existence. Still, this past experience is with me.

During the experience of inner depth, I abandoned my power to formulate and express ideas, and I gave it to an unfamiliar precious source deep within me. I let go of my tendency to judge and opinionate, and instead I resonated with the voices of my companions and of my own reality. I was no longer an independent thinker, but became part of a greater realm, like a wave among other waves in an ocean. Later, weeks or months after the experience, I understood that as long as I am still in touch with my inner depth, I would remain ultimately ethical, and the distinction between what is inside me and outside me would not be sharp and distancing. For example, I often feel touched by a secret fragility of the world around me, which shows itself as naked and vulnerable, giving me a sense of great confidence: I am responsible, and I should change myself completely in the face of such presence.

For a long time after my first retreat I felt myself unusually open to the world, and empathic and kind towards other people. This made me think that inner depth must have given birth to the great masterpieces of world culture. During the Brando retreat I discovered in myself a sacred element, an infinite spiritual treasure, usually guarded by my inner darkness. It connects me to ultimate reality, perhaps through the creative act. As the Russian religious philosopher Nikolai Berdyaev said in his book *The Meaning of the Creative Act*,[13] first published in 1916: "In the mystery of creativity, the infinite nature of the human being is revealed, and his highest vocation takes place."

---

13. Nikolai Berdyaev, *The Meaning of the Creative Act*, Collier Books, New York, 1955, Chapter 3.

PRECIOUS MOMENTS

Stefania Giordano

The aim of Deep Philosophy, as I see it, is to enrich and deepen people's lives. Its task is not to cure psychological problems or alleviate distress, because we do not regard life as revolving around the issues of sickness and health. The goal of deep philosophers is not to find a cure for personal problems, but to search for a glimpse of light in the dark forest, to find the precious element in our lives.

What is this element of "light" or "preciousness"? It is not a theoretical construct, an abstract invention, a speculation. It is something that participants feel strongly as a powerful encounter with something valuable and meaningful, a sense of being filled with new spiritual richness and wisdom, an openness to the infinite treasures of philosophical thought.

In this chapter I would like to offer my reflections on this preciousness.

Precious moments in a Deep Philosophy session

In a typical Deep Philosophy session, we use various procedures and techniques in order to abandon our normal psychological structures and get in touch with a deeper level of our being, the source of the self. There, deep within ourselves, a fountain keeps flowing with the plenitude of inspiration and wisdom, even when we are not in touch with it.

How do we seek this fountain?

Our starting point is always a philosophical text, which serves us as a source of inspiration, a muse that can lead us towards our inner depth. We usually start a session by working together to understand the selected text and explore some of its many meanings. But we do not do so academically, we do not limit ourselves to abstract thinking that involves only our analytic mind. We think and interact from our entire being – body and soul and heart, like one unitary organism. To do so, we usually use a procedure we call "interpretive reading," in which we read the text several times while we resonate with it and with other participants who spoke before us. The text suggests a certain landscape of ideas, and we enter into the new landscape, while, metaphorically speaking, we hold hands in togetherness. For me, understanding in togetherness is the first precious moment in the session.

I think of the process that leads to such a precious moment as if our little familiar selves rise and enter a higher self, guided by the philosophical words. At that moment, you can see your individual life against the background of the infinite ocean of ideas and reality. You can see yourself not only in the narrow domain of your small existence, not just in terms of your specific biographical conditions, but as part of the greater realm of life which extends far beyond your narrow world of experiences. For me, the connection between the small self and the higher self is the first element of preciousness in the session.

My second precious moment usually appears in the following exercise. After we have understood the text, we sometimes select from it a sentence and repeat it again and again in a circle. The result is a kind of chanting, or what we call *Ruminatio* (a term borrowed from Catholic monastic tradition), which produces a sort of precious music that gives the entire group a very powerful atmosphere. The words stop being ordinary words, and we "taste" them as if they were a sacred food, a nourishment for the spirit. Such a precious moment enlarges and broadens our worldview beyond the usual meaning of words, and it gives us a sense of being greater than our usual self.

A third moment of preciousness takes place later in the session, and it is the true heart of Deep Philosophy. After we have understood the text and have chanted selected sentences from it, the facilitator invites the participants to reflect on a small moment which they experienced recently. The participants fall silent for a few moments and glance at the text, and the words evoke in each one a personal memory.

The remembered incident does not have to be especially dramatic or life-changing. On the contrary, it is better to choose a seemingly unimportant little moment, a tiny segment of the daily flow the events. At first, the memory might seem insignificant, but as the session progresses, it usually turns out to contain abundance of meanings and wondrous surprises.

The result of this exercise is a kind of dance between the philosophical idea and one's personal life, and this dance is a fountain of preciousness. Each participant oscillates between the text and his or her selected personal moment, between ideas and life, between being and Being. We then realize that by attending to tiny moments in our life, and with the aid of deep ideas, life can reveal itself as full of meanings and preciousness. In this sense, the session serves as a space in which bits of precious beauty are magnified.

Looking at the session as a whole, it is clear that, unlike philosophical counseling, we do not try to detect psychological mechanisms or patterns, nor do we try to modify an emotional or behavioral pattern into something better. Our goal is to enrich life by helping it get in touch with the depth. And an important way to do so is to experience those precious moments. These moments are transformative because they open a door to the depth. Cultivating beauty as in a Zen garden means educating the self to embrace the wonder. The creation of a string of meaningful moments makes the person feel pregnant with a kind of plenitude. Every pearl of this powerful jewel is a drop of preciousness.

Different faces of preciousness

As I said before, there are three main precious moments in a standard session of Deep Philosophy. Let me point out that they each have a different kind of "magical" power:

The first precious moment, as we have seen, happens at the beginning of the session, when the participants enter the philosophical landscape suggested by the writer. Here the power of the moment consists of a sense of going beyond my boundaries: resonating together with my companions and discovering new unexpected meanings that enlarge and enrich my little world.

The second precious moment takes place when participants chant together selected sentences from the text, repeating them again and again. The power of this moment comes from a sense of going down into my innermost being, namely my inner depth, and listening to it as it expresses its insights. I no longer think and speak from my usual discursive mind but from a deeper source within me.

In the third moment, the participants connect a philosophical idea to little moments from their lives. The sense of preciousness comes from the discovery that my concrete life is connected to broader philosophical meanings. My finite existence become a little fragment in the bigger realm of life and of reality.

These three are evidently different experiences, and yet they are all different faces of the same thing – a sense of preciousness. What is the common element in these experiences?

I suggest that the sense of preciousness, in all its forms, involves abandoning our ordinary consciousness, which is limited, fragmented, and mechanical, and attaining instead a sense of wholeness. In this state I relate from my whole being to life as a whole. This is why we sometimes use meditative or centering exercises during the session, often at the beginning. Such techniques help us abandon our usual state of mind and embrace a different way of being and thinking.

Concluding the session

We end a Deep Philosophy session without a definite solution or resolution. We do not solve psychological issues, we do not analyze psychological structures, we do not try to change behaviors or emotional patterns. Although some of these may happen during the session, this is not our goal. The goal is to make our life more deeply philosophical.

We emerge from a session after a journey into our inner depth. The precious insights and moments which we have experienced give us a deep sense of plenitude, togetherness, and inner silence. The experience of precious moments continues to resonate within us. Precious moments are transformative – they gradually change our orientation to life and make it broader and deeper.

Let me conclude with Marcus Aurelius' very appropriate words: *"Look inside yourself. Inside is the fountain of Good, and it will always bubble up, if you always dig."*[14]

---

14. Marcus Aurelius, *Meditations*, Prometheus Books, Amherst NY, 1991, Book VII 59.

THE PHILOSOPHICAL POLYPHONY

Sebastian Drobny

> "*Let him be to me a spirit. A message, a thought, a sincerity, a glance from him, I want, but not news, nor pottage. I can get politics, and chat, and neighborly conveniences from cheaper companions. Should not the society of my friend be to me poetic, pure, universal, and great as nature itself? Ought I to feel that our tie is profane in comparison with yonder bar of cloud that sleeps on the horizon, or that clump of waving grass that divides the brook?*"
>
> Ralph Waldo Emerson[15]

I never had this kind of friendship until recently, when I started to experience it with my esteemed companions of the Deep Philosophy group. Isn't it strange? After months of working together in online sessions, meetings and retreats, we barely know anything about each other's daily life. We don't know which kind of music others like, what their favorite TV series is, or what a day at their workplace looks like. We grew up in different countries and cultures. But our shared contemplative journeys and our joint exploration of our inner depth did

---

15. "Friendship," *Essays and English Traits*, Collier, New York, 1909. (Originally published in his *Essays, First Series* in 1841.)

something to us as a group. We became friends. Our friendship seems to me as great as nature itself. It is an ongoing fountain of inspiration, trust and appreciation. I believe that the growth of our friendship is largely due to the "polyphonic" atmosphere of Deep Philosophy.

"Philosophical polyphony" is our main way of interacting with each other when we practice Deep Philosophy. Polyphony occurs when we express our understanding of life without judging each other. We give voice to our own "music," so to speak, without agreeing or disagreeing with the "music" of our companions. In this chapter I would like to explain how this kind of discourse works.

What is polyphony in a philosophical discourse?

In the field of music, polyphony means that multiple voices join together to create a single musical piece. The different voices are not opposed to each other but merge into a new whole. Polyphonic music can serve as a metaphor for the way different philosophical ideas, voiced side by side in a Deep Philosophy session, can interact with each other.

Speaking in polyphony means that the participants do not evaluate each other's words or argue with each other. Like jazz musicians playing together, they do not play against each other but rather with each other, in togetherness. Listening to one another, they are inspired to create their own musical tunes in harmony with the others. In mainstream philosophy, it is common to analyze each other's ideas and develop arguments for or against each other. But if I do this in a Deep Philosophy session, I would enter a judgmental state of mind, and would be distancing myself from my own source of ideas – and from my inner depth. Critical discussion may be acceptable in scientific and academic discourse, but in Deep Philosophy the participants – our "jazz musicians" – must avoid it. For the duration of the session, there is no right or wrong.

But if so, then where is philosophy in a polyphonic discourse? The answer is, in part, that the session revolves around a selected philosophical text which addresses a philosophical issue, in other words a fundamental issue about life. Furthermore, the participants use various procedures and exercises to develop and express their own philosophical ideas about that fundamental issue.

This does not mean that "anything goes" and that any idea is just good as another. As in Jazz, there are accepted musical structures for playing in a well-sounding way, and these structures help the musicians play together in the same "language." Just as musicians do not play by themselves in isolation from their fellow musicians, Deep Philosophy participants do not isolate themselves in their respective personal opinions. They are attentive to each other and resonate with each other. Without this sense of togetherness, no facilitator or common text would be able to unify the different voices into a common polyphonic philosophy. With a sense of togetherness, the polyphonic group-process is enriched by the different philosophical voices which inspire each other and help the participants explore their authentic philosophical conceptions.

What is a philosophical "voice"?

To demonstrate what I mean by a "philosophical voice," let us look at how polyphony can be created from two different thinkers with different views about the same issue: the meaning of the other person, or the Other. The French philosopher Emmanuel Levinas[16] explains that when I encounter another person, this other person is for me a complete otherness, an alterity for which I have an inevitable responsibility. The encounter with the Other is a most fundamental experience; it is more primordial than even our self-consciousness or consciousness-of things. The Other appears to me

---

16. Emmanuel Levinas, "Ethics as a First Philosophy" *The Levinas Reader*, Blackwell, Oxford, 1993, pages 75-87.

through his face, and the face is exposed, naked, vulnerable. This vulnerable face calls me: "Don't kill me!" In this sense, the potential death of the Other appears on his face. Therefore, the face is an ethical command that is directed at me. I am responsible for the Other, unconditionally responsible.

We find a very different perspective when we look at the Spanish philosopher José Ortega y Gasset.[17] In his account, the idea of the Other's vulnerability and my fundamental responsibility to him plays almost no part. On the contrary, the other person appears in my life-world as a danger to me. To make this concrete, Ortega asks us to imagine walking at night when suddenly you hear footsteps. "Who is there?!" You are no longer careless and relaxed but on guard and cautious. The reason you react this way is that the other person is a hidden inwardness. I cannot see his thoughts, his emotions, his intentions. This inwardness can be revealed to me through his body, his face and eyes, but only partly. I can never be sure what he thinks or feels, and how he is going to react to me.

Just like Levinas and Ortega, each one of us has a specific philosophical "voice" or conception of the Other, whether conscious or unconscious. Of course, none of us is Levinas or Ortega; most likely my

---

17. José Ortega y Gasset, *Man and People*, Norton, New York, 1963, Chapter 7, pages 139-170.

conception differs significantly from theirs. Whatever our conceptions are, they have a profound impact on our personal lives. They express themselves in our actions, feelings and thoughts, and our entire attitude to ourselves, to our world, and to life.

During a Deep Philosophy session, participants give voice to their conceptions, while carefully listening to each other and thinking about them from their inner depth. When I share my thoughts with others, everything that has been said is still present, and it resonates with my own thoughts. The result is like doing a musical jam session together. If I play together with John, I play my own music. The same is true if I play with Simon. But my music will be different in each jam session, because our interactions will be different.

So far, we have seen the value of not judging the rightness or wrongness of other philosophical voices. We have seen that in Deep Philosophy sessions it is important to discover one's authentic voice – one's own "music." How can we ensure that participants will think about the philosophical ideas that are authentically theirs, and not just copy somebody else's ideas or talk in the abstract? In other words, how can we ensure that participants will speak from their inner depth? As we will see, the structure, the polyphony and the facilitator of the session play key roles.

Polyphonic procedures

In an ordinary session, the philosophical polyphony is composed of several "voices": the voice of the philosophical text, the voice of your own attitudes and experiences, and the voices of the other participants in the session. Jazz is not just several players playing side by side for themselves. Coordination and interaction among the players are essential. How do we interact polyphonically in Deep Philosophy, either with a text or with our companions? Let me give several examples of procedures that create polyphony.

One example is a procedure we call "interpretive reading," which is used to get acquainted with a selected text and reflect on it. The group focuses on a short passage in the text, usually about three-four sentences, and each participant in his or her turn reads the passage out loud, while occasionally adding a brief interpretation of a word or sentence in the text. Participants never express agreement or disagreement with previous readers ("I agree with your explanation of the first sentence"), and never even talk about previous interpretations ("As Alicia said…). They are only allowed to read the same passage again, together with their own brief interpretations. While doing so, they are encouraged to "resonate" with previous readings: to repeat a previous interpretation, or to elaborate on what has been said, to complement it with a new idea, or go in a different direction altogether. After a round or two, the participants continue to the next passage and again read it out loud in an interpretive way, one after the other, until the end of the text.

The result of this procedure is a polyphony of interpretations – a cluster of different voices, each one emphasizing different ideas, but all of them revolving around the same text and resonating with each other. The group now has a rich understanding of the text. The words of the text are enriched with an array of meanings, some complementing each other while others offering alternative understandings.

A second example of a polyphonic procedure is what we call "precious speaking." We use this procedure to express our own ideas while resonating with the ideas of others. It is also designed to prevent us from chatting and from analytic or superficial thinking, and it gives space to individual thoughts and insights to arise from the inner depth.

In this procedure, each participant is invited to give voice to a thought or experience, either according to the sitting order or freely without turns

– but in one sentence only. Participants are instructed to express each word as if it was precious, as if it was a valuable gift to the group. They must avoid repetitions, redundancies, or gap-fillers such as "In my opinion…," "It is important to remember that…," "I'd like to repeat what she said…," or "It just came into my mind that…"

The way we talk influences our state of mind. As the participants start picking their words carefully and speaking in a condensed and precise way, their inner attitude changes too. It is no longer an attitude of discussing and expressing opinions, because it becomes gentle and attentive to each word and to others. Participants are no longer inclined to judge or comment on the other voices, but rather to resonate with them. For example, they may repeat a companion's phrase, or add a new word to a previous phrase, develop more fully a fragment of thought, or be inspired by another participant's words to create a new thought. In several rounds of such "precious speaking," the group as a whole speaks. You don't need to worry about whether your friends would judge your idea as immature or faulty, because you are not standing in front of their judging eyes – you are shoulder to shoulder with them, creating together. The thoughts flow freely, evolving from one thought to another, without interrupting the contemplative atmosphere.

Finally, I would like to describe a third procedure called "resonating with a personal experience." An important aim of Deep Philosophy is to enrich our everyday moments with the help of philosophical ideas. A powerful way to do so is to ask participants to select a small event or situation which they had experienced recently, and then to let it resonate with a philosophical text and with other participants' voices. This brings up new words and understandings, evoked from our inner depth, about this seemingly small but meaningful everyday moment: a brief random encounter with somebody in the supermarket, for example, or a moment of noticing the texture of dough between my fingers as I was baking bread.

We start this procedure by first reflecting on a philosophical text, possibly through the "interpretive reading" procedure. After familiarizing ourselves with the main ideas, participants are asked to think about a personal experience which reminds them of an idea or sentence in the text. After a few minutes, a volunteer describes his or her experience briefly, perhaps in no more than a sentence or two. The facilitator may ask a few clarification questions, while the others listen closely. But the main work is not in getting the details correctly, but rather adding new meanings to the experience. To do so, all the participants try to immerse themselves in this experience as if it was their own, and as if it is happening right now. In several rounds of "precious speaking" they listen carefully to their inner depth and give voice to the insights which bubble up from within. These "bubbles" provide new ideas and meanings to the experience, producing a concert of different voices that sing polyphonically about the same event, which now becomes enriched with new perspectives.

Another person may reveal something meaningful in our own experience, which was not in our sight and yet is worth considering. Therefore, the procedure of "resonating with a personal experience" enables us to go beyond our own self-closed world. We open ourselves to a richer reality, to the fullness and multiplicity of the outer world.

An example of a session

Let me demonstrate the power of polyphony by giving an imaginary example. The session focuses on a couple of pages from the essay "Why do we write" by the Spanish philosopher Maria Zambrano,[18] in which she argues that we write in order to preserve an inner space that is free from the continuous flow of time. Normally we are lost in the flow of moments

---

18. Maria Zambrano, "Por qué se escribe"("Why does one write"), *Hacia un Saber Sobre el Alma* (*Towards Knowledge of the Soul*), Alianza, Fernandez Ciudad, 2008, pages 35-44.

and events. We may momentarily regain our awareness and freedom by thinking and talking in words, but that moment will immediately disappear into the past, covered by subsequent moments. We feel we have to defend our inner solitude in order not to lose ourselves, and that is why we write. By writing we stop the flow of time, so to speak, we create a separate space that is not washed away by this flow, that is outside time, and that is truly ours.

In our example, there are three participants: Marco the facilitator, Sylvia and Klara. Zambrano's text is not easy, and Marco knows that he should give his two companions some time to read it, reflect on it, and acquaint themselves with its basic ideas. He could have given a little lecture, but that would invite analytic thinking and judgement of right and wrong, and it would go against the contemplative spirit. He therefore starts with the procedure of interpretive reading, focusing on the first few lines:

"Writing is defending the solitude in which one is. It is an action which only sprouts from real isolation, but a communicable isolation, one in which the distance from all concrete things makes it possible to discover the relations among them."

Marco reads this short fragment slowly and out loud. Since he is already familiar with the text, he adds his own interpretations as he goes along, offering his two listeners his understanding of the text.

"*Writing is defending the solitude in which one is,*" he reads, then adds, "I have to defend my solitude. Solitude is not naturally given to me, and I must work to achieve it. Writing is *an action which only sprouts from isolation* – it is born only if I enter my inner world. But this isolation does not mean that I am in a void, because it is a *communicable isolation*. By distancing myself *from all concrete things* I can discover *relations among them*, hidden relations and hidden meanings."

Notice that Marco is not talking *about* the text but *with* the text, in parallel with it, resonating with Maria Zambrano. He speaks in the first person – about himself (and he invites the others to do the same), in order to internalize the text and speak from it.

Marco now signals to Sylvia, and she reads the same sentences while interpreting it in her own words. That does not mean that she has to invent a completely new interpretation – she is free to repeat words which Marco has already used, to reformulate them, or simply to read the text without interpretation if she cannot think of anything to add.

Klara is the next to read, and after she finishes, Marcos continues to the second fragment of the text and the three start a new round of interpretive reading. Then they continue to the third fragment, and then to the fourth. The entire procedure takes about twenty minutes. At no point do they analyze the text, discuss it, correct each other, agree or disagree. The important point is not academic accuracy but developing a rich polyphony of personal understandings.

Their repetitive reading flows rhythmically, and the three are now submerged in the text. They notice the beginning of a gentle contemplative state of mind. Marco now wants to go deeper into some of the ideas that came up, and in order to preserve the polyphonic contemplative atmosphere he chooses the procedure of precious speaking.

He invites the two others to share an idea, whether from the text or from their own thoughts, that touched them during the reading – but to express it in precious speaking, in a few precise words. You may use the words of the text, he explains, or your own words.

Sylvia says: "Writing is defending my solitude." Marco follows by saying: "My isolation needs protection." Then Klara: "When I speak words, I am disintegrated, but in writing I recollect myself." A few more rounds of precious speaking continue to develop these threads of ideas, as the participants listen to each other and resonate with each other's words, creating a polyphonic concert.

"Very good," Marco says, "we now have a rich network of ideas. Let us connect it to our own personal experiences." He asks for a volunteer to share very briefly a relevant personal experience. Sylvia volunteers.

"A couple of weeks ago," she says, trying to speak as briefly as she can, "I had an unpleasant conversation with my boyfriend. I told him that he was being bossy with me, giving me advice, interrogating me, lecturing to me, as if he was in charge of running my life." Sylvia falls silent, then adds, "So when we read in Zambrano about protecting my inner solitude against the flood of life, I recalled this conversation. I remembered how his many words swamped me, and I lost connection with my inner space."

"Thank you, Sylvia," Marco says. "I appreciate your honesty and trust. There are probably many more details to this story, but we are not doing psychology here. We don't want to analyze you or solve your problems. You gave us a brief glimpse of this event – let us work with what we have and use our imagination to enrich it with new meanings."

Marco starts a few rounds of resonating with Sylvia's experience, in the precious speaking mode. They speak in the first person as if they had experienced Sylvia's story by themselves, without trying to be true to the facts.

Marco is the first to speak, and he focuses on Zambrano's expression "communicable isolation" which fascinates him: "I want to be in communicable isolation – isolated and yet communicating."

Klara, scanning the text, resonates with him: "I need my separateness so I can communicate with you, so I can be close to you."

Sylvia, who has been listening attentively, feels the words coming spontaneously out of her mouth: "In isolation I reconquer myself, in isolation I reconquer my lost ability to connect."

Marco, in his second turn, adds. "Solitude is part of togetherness: I want to be in solitude together with you."

A few more rounds follow, and the sentences gradually become more spontaneous and creative. The result is a rich symphony of ideas about Sylvia's experience, enriched by new meanings from Zambrano's ideas. Needless to say, these ideas do not add up to one single thesis about Sylvia – this is not a psychological analysis of her experience. It is a creative choir of meanings about human life and human relationships, which goes beyond Sylvia's particular personal story. As Marco remarks at the conclusion of the session, the role of this creative choir is wisdom and growth: to teach us to see the rich horizons of human existence.

Conclusion – the power of polyphony

At this point we leave the session, because we have already glimpsed the power of polyphony in Deep Philosophy. Polyphony gives us a vivid access to a philosophical text and to its broader world of meanings. Polyphonic procedures, such as the three described above – including their rhythm, their focus, and their contemplative atmosphere – change our state of mind and allow us to enter the world of the text and explore it from an inner perspective. The participants' polyphonic voices fill the group's mental space with creative ideas and personal experiences.

Deep Philosophy provides very rewarding experiences, but it is not intended just for intellectual pleasure. It connects us deeply with substantial aspects of life. It also enriches and deepens the nature of the philosophical discourse. Without expressing our personal experiences and our inner depth, the philosophical discourse would remain (to use Bergson's words) "dead leaves on the water of a pond," devoid of personal connection. As Bergson tells us, we are normally aware only of the surface of life – of fixed ideas and emotions that can be easily described. But beneath this familiar surface, our inner life is in a constant flux of infinite qualities and meanings, like an ongoing, creative, flowing symphony that includes our entire being. In Deep Philosophy we wander, side by side with our companions, beyond our self-enclosed world and open ourselves to reality, to its fullness and its many faces.

WHAT IS RECOLLECTION? [19]

Sergey Borisov

In our work to cultivate our inner depth, our Deep Philosophy group has developed a variety of activities and exercises. Many of them are practiced in small groups, but not all of them. One important exercise, called Recollection, is practiced individually. You practice it during the week, usually for a few minutes at a time, in order to step out of the busy activity of the day, reflect, and reconnect to yourselves and your inner depth. Here the two meanings of the English word "recollection" are united: The word means remembering, but it also means collecting yourself again (re-collecting), in other words finding yourself again after being lost in everyday activity.

Recollection has simple guidelines: Several times during the week you stop whatever you are doing, step out of your ordinary activity, and for several minutes listen inwardly to deep insights that may arise in you or float in your mind. To facilitate the

---

19. This article was prepared as part of the RFBR project No. 17-33-00021, "Theory and Practice of Philosophical Counseling: Comparative Approach."

process, you may read gently a short text from a recent contemplative session, or recite several times a sentence that you had copied on paper, or sit down and contemplate for a few minutes, write a sentence slowly and gently, and so on. Afterwards, or at the end of the day, you write down the insights that arose in your mind. At the end of the week, you may send the week's recollections to a companion – your "reader," who might respond and comment in a non-judgmental way.

The rules of Recollection are, then, simple and flexible. But the main thing happens internally, within us.

The experience of recollecting

In recollection we retreat from the world into a quiet inner space, and we experience ourselves resonating with our reality and communicating with it. This typically requires being in silence and solitude for a few minutes. We then feel that past thoughts and experiences start emerging from the depths of our mind into our consciousness. Normally, our mind keeps these memories scattered and fragmentary: the important is mixed with the unimportant, the significant with the insignificant. Recollection serves to integrate these scattered memories, bring them to light, and give them clarity.

But recollection cannot be practiced anywhere and at any time. It may work, for example, in those moments when, tired of work or of everyday worries, we sit alone, or walk quietly, or simply look around, gently resting our eyes on one thing then another. In such moments, our attention changes: whereas previously it was directed outwards towards things and people, now it attends inwardly. Our inner listening opens up, and it begins to pick up the voices of our reality. Everything that is secondary and irrelevant fades into the background, and in the foreground appears a thought, an insight, an experience that is full of deep meanings.

This deep meaning cannot always be expressed in words, even when it fills our entire being. We can simply listen to its voice, while immersing ourselves in the feeling of belonging to the universe. We can enter into dialogue with this voice, so that our experience of participating in reality takes on a form of thought. This voice may also become embodied in our own voice and express itself in our mind in a discursive or poetic way. As a result, our ordinary way of speaking and thinking changes: Instead of describing our inner state from the perspective of an external observer, we now speak from our inner depth, from the depth of our experience, trying to resonate with the voices of reality. In this process, we re-collect ourselves and integrate our thoughts and feelings into a single whole.

Recollection may have different sources. It may bring up a memory of a significant insight we have not previously noticed in the midst of our busy everyday activity. It may be based on actual events that happened to us recently, which now surface to our consciousness when we reflect, carefully and gently, on the various episodes of the day. Recollection helps give meaning to these episodes, and this meaning can be embodied in a new thought or idea. Alternatively, recollection can be based on a philosophical text which we had read earlier, or which we are reading now, as we resonate with its basic ideas. These ideas can serve as a door to the depth through which reality penetrates us.

Examples of my recollections

The following are examples of my own recollections, which I conducted at the beginning of 2019. This was shortly after I participated in group-contemplation on a text by the German-American philosopher and theologian Paul Tillich. His ideas touched me, and I decided to use some of his writings for my recollections. (The texts I used can be found on the Agora website.) Notice that my recollections were not intended to explain what Tillich said, but to use his text as a seed for my own insights and thoughts.

Recollections on Paul Tillich's *The Courage to Be*

Tuesday

I sit on my armchair in front of the fireplace. Through the window I can see the starry night. I look at the fire for a long time, and suddenly a phrase from Tillich floats into my mind:

"... non-being is a part of one's own being."

And I realize: Everything I ever had in mind, everything I have been accustomed to, everything I love, all that is valuable to me – all this will end. I look at myself, and I see myself sitting silently at my desk. I sense my body. But I can also feel very clearly how my time is passing, the time of my life. And I understand that this flow of time carries me along to non-being, to nothingness.

Wednesday

I wake up in the morning. Instead of rushing to start the day, I stop and listen to myself. Again a phrase from Tillich appears in my mind:

"... anxiety is existential in the sense that it belongs to existence as such."

Anxiety is always with me – this is the main state of my existence. I am going to give a lecture soon, and my anxiety is with me. What I worry about is not that I will forget something, or fail to do something – I worry about myself as a whole, about my defenseless existence. I worry about what I am, but also about how others, or the world, will accept the way I am.

Thursday

The workday is over. I am driving home. The evening lights of the city pass by through the car window. I am satisfied with this day. I understand what Tillich means when he writes:

"Courage is self-affirmation 'in spite of', namely in spite of non-being."

I tell myself: Let go of anxiety, let go of fear... My courage is not fleeing from my anxiety, not denying it, not trying to change myself (in other words, being an Other). My courage is asserting myself. Recently I was offered to participate in a certain project. My first impulse was to refuse. Nevertheless, contrary to this impulse, I said Yes. Why? Well, why not? When I say No, I am in effect saying that I don't exist. And when I say Yes, I affirm that I am, I exist, I am alive.

Friday

I read a page from Tillich's book *The Courage to Be*, and a sentence attracts my attention:

"Without this self-affirmation, life could not be preserved or increased."

I understand: In my self-affirmation there is a thirst for life. I say to myself: Why are you sad? What's wrong? Later, I sit at the dinner table. Here is my wife, here are my children. All of a sudden I feel joy filling me, the joy that they need me, that they are talking to me, and also about themselves. But most importantly – they are WITH ME. I turn my full attention to them. And it strikes me deeply that in this unique moment I understand my purpose in life.

Saturday

Evening. I turn off the computer, but I keep sitting by my desk. It is time to reflect on the day. I wonder whether I have achieved what I had read in Tillich:

"…the balance of fear and courage."

There is a boundary between fear and courage, where I always try to balance the two opposites. Today I spoke with a certain person, and I needed courage to overcome my fear and refuse his request. I could not fulfill this request; I knew that. I knew I should not even give him any illusory hope. But to do this, I had to overcome my fear that he would consider me bad and insensitive. Somehow I found the courage to refuse him. Had I not done so, there would have been deception and self-deception.

Recollections on Tillich's *The Dynamics of Faith*

Wednesday

I sit in silence in front of the fireplace, summarizing the day in my mind. I remember Tillich's explanation of how symbols, as opposed to conventional signs, can take us to different levels of reality. I recall the sentence:

"...signs do not participate in the reality of that to which they point, while symbols do."

My mind wanders to the depth of the symbol of hospitality. I recall how I wanted to help a certain person, but did not know how to offer him my help. He was not a close friend, but after I invited him for dinner, I discovered his unusual, interesting personality. For me he was transformed, opened up, and he turned out to be a very special and deep person. My life has become richer.

I now recall another phrase by Tillich:

"...a symbol opens up levels of reality which otherwise are closed for us."

This man gave me a collection of his poems. I knew that he was writing poetry, but I did not suspect that his poems were so beautiful and deep. Previously, had somebody shown me his poems, I would not have believed that they were his. How deceptive can appearances be...

Thursday

While reading a poetry book, I feel resonating with Tillich's thoughts about the symbol:

"There are within us dimensions of which we cannot become aware except through symbols."

This book of poems has revealed a lot to me about myself. I especially liked one poem which speaks about the work of a sculptor who uses two materials: clay – a symbol of generosity and variability; and marble – a symbol of constancy and rigor. These symbols are transferred into the relationship between people: "the clay of meeting" and "the marble of separation." I am inspired by it.

"… Symbols cannot be invented," says Tillich.

Another poem touches me, a poem called "Death." It strikes me that death is a symbol too, because we don't actually know anything about it. Yet, death exists for us symbolically. What does death symbolize? It symbolizes uncertainty and inevitability, and it indicates that all this must be accepted.

ABOUT THE AUTHORS

Massimiliano Bavieri is an Italian philosopher, pianist, translator and teacher. He received his Master's degree in piano from the Music Institute "Luigi Boccherini" in Lucca, and a second Master's degree in Philosophy from the University of Pisa. He joined the movement of philosophical practice in 2007, and in 2017 took part in a philosophical contemplative retreat organized by Ran Lahav in Liguria. In 2019 he became a full member of the Deep Philosophy Group. He taught piano in secondary school, and since 2007 has been teaching Italian as a foreign language at the center for adult education in Lucca. He is also a translator, and has published his Italian translations of several German philosophical essays.

Sergey Borisov is a doctor of philosophy and professor at South Ural State University (Chelyabinsk, Russia). Since 2014 he has been active in the international movement of philosophical practice. He conducts a philosophical cafe in Chelyabinsk, he also works in the Philosophy for Children program at a Montessori center. He is the head of the scientific project "Theory and practice of philosophical consulting: comparative approach," which received financial support from the Russian Foundation for Basic Research.

Francesca D'Uva studied philosophy at D'Annunzio University in Chieti, Italy, and graduated in philosophy in 2015 with a thesis in philosophy of religion. She studied philosophical practice at the Parresìa School in Bologna. In recent years she has been working in a variety of areas, social, educational, and technical. She joined the Deep Philosophy group in 2019, and is now involved, among other things, in the organization of the group's activities and retreats in Italy.

Sebastian Drobny is a German certified biotechnologist, currently living in Austria. In 2015 he received his BSc at the University of Applied Sciences Esslingen, and then worked as specialist for testing methods at the headquarters of Paul Hartmann Ag in Heidenheim, Germany. Since then he has been working as a tutor at the department of ethics in the sciences and technologies for universities in the state of Baden-Württemberg in Germany. In 2017 he started his Bachelor's studies of philosophy at the University of Vienna in Austria. Out of his love of nature he is also working as gardener.

Stefania Giordano is an Italian philosophical practitioner since 2007. After finishing her Master's Degree in Philosophy with a thesis on philosophical counseling, she studied philosophical practice at the Sicof School in Rome, where she now works in administration, management, and teaching. She has facilitated many philosophical cafés, philosophical groups, and one-to-one sessions, has worked as a philosophical practitioner in high schools, and has written articles for specialized magazines. She is a family mediator and operator of a women's center crisis as an expert on gender violence. She is now taking a second Master's degree in Educational Science.

Ran Lahav has been internationally active in the field of philosophical practice since 1992. He grew up in Israel, and then moved to the USA and received in 1989 his PhD in philosophy and Master's in Psychology from the University of Michigan. He taught philosophy at several universities in Israel and the USA, and gave the first university course in the world on philosophical counseling at Haifa University in Israel, which he taught for over ten years. In 1994 he envisioned and co-organized the First International Conference on Philosophical Counseling. He has given numerous workshops and presentations around the world, and has published books and articles on philosophy and philosophical practice, as well as novels and spirituality books in English and Hebrew.

Kirill Rezvushkin is a candidate of sciences (Russian equivalent of PhD), an associate professor at the Department of Philosophy of South Ural State University (Chelyabinsk, Russia). In 2009 he received his specialist diploma (equivalent to the Master's degree) in Russian Philology, and in 2016 his specialist diploma in history at Chelyabinsk State University. His dissertation on philosophy, which he defended in 2015, was about authenticity.

Michele Zese is an Italian philosophical practitioner, who gives philosophical thinking activities to small children, as well as to teenagers in schools. He received his Master's degree in philosophy from the University of Turin, specializing in philosophy of mind, and in 2016 received a second Master's in philosophical counseling at Sicof School. In 2017 he joined Ran Lahav in organizing philosophical contemplative retreats. In one of these retreats he took part in the creation of the Deep Philosophy group.